GUITAR FRETBOARD
MEMORY MAGIC

PAINLESSLY MEMORIZE ALL THE NOTES
ON YOUR NECK FOREVER FOR INSTANT RECALL

SAMURAI FINGERS

INCLUDES
FREE VIDEO COMPANION COURSE

NICK MORRISON
WWW.GUITARDOJO.CA

© Copyright 2020 Nick Morrison — All rights reserved.

The content contained within this book may not be reproduced, duplicated or transmitted without direct written permission from the author or the publisher.

Under no circumstances will any blame or legal responsibility be held against the publisher, or author, for any damages, reparation, or monetary loss due to the information contained within this book. Either directly or indirectly. You are responsible for your own choices, actions, and results.

Legal Notice:
This book is copyright protected. This book is only for personal use. You cannot amend, distribute, sell, use, quote or paraphrase any part, or the content within this book, without the consent of the author or publisher.

Disclaimer Notice:
Please note the information contained within this document is for educational and entertainment purposes only. All effort has been executed to present accurate, up to date, and reliable, complete information. No warranties of any kind are declared or implied. Readers acknowledge that the author is not engaging in the rendering of legal, financial, medical or professional advice.

By reading this document, the reader agrees that under no circumstances is the author responsible for any losses, direct or indirect, which are incurred as a result of the use of the information contained within this document, including, but not limited to, — errors, omissions, or inaccuracies.

FOR FURTHER HELP, LEARNING AND DEVELOPMENT:

Be sure to check out Nicks' Youtube Channel where he posts weekly lesson videos, tips, tricks and more. You can find it at www.youtube.com/samuraifingers

Please be sure to join the Samurai Fingers Guitar Dojo on FaceBook for even more free tips, tricks, lesson videos, exclusive content and an entire community of guitar players just like you! There is always someone around and available to answer questions, provide feedback or even just share a "like" on a video that's posted! You can find us on FB at www.facebook.com/groups/theguitardojo!

FREEBIES!
Head over to www.guitardojo.ca where you can sign up for my email list and get instant access to your very own FREE pdf copy of my "Essential Chords and Scales" eBook — this is an invaluable resource for both the beginning guitarist and seasoned professional alike! It's full of all the most common chords and scales in every key! Seriously, it's such a great tool to have printed off and handy, or even just keep it as a resource on your iphone/ipad/tablet or computer.

PLUS!
You'll also get instant access to the FREE video companion lesson that goes with this book! (instructions will come in the email for how/where to stream the video)

CONTENTS

About the Author:

Nick Morrison is a professional musician, composer, teacher, writer, narrator/voice actor, YouTube creator, actor and music/media consultant from Calgary Alberta. He has toured throughout the United States, Canada and Japan as a guitarist, worked as a session musician and writer/composer for Warner Bros, Google, Universal Studios, Sony, MTV, ABC, NBC, HGTV, HBO among others.

He was educated at The Berklee College of Music in Boston Mass, where he studied guitar performance and music business management.

In 2020 he began writing guitar instructional books and will continue to bring his love of the instrument to as many people around the world as possible.

INTRODUCTION 6

FIRST THINGS FIRST 8

EXERCISE #1 10

EXERCISE #2 12

EXERCISE #3 14

EXERCISE #4 16

EXERCISE #5 18

EXERCISE #6 20

THAT'S A WRAP! 22

APPENDIX

NOTES ON THE FRETBOARD 24

BLANK CHORD
DIAGRAMS FOR YOUR USE 40

BLANK STAFF/TAB PAPER
FOR YOUR USE 46

INTRODUCTION

Would you like to be able to see all the notes on your guitar fretboard so you can instantly know where an "F" is on the 4th string, or a "G" for that matter on the 5th string or any other note at all?

Then this method is for you —
I will show you how to do just that!
This is fast, easy, fun and you will memorize ALL of the notes on your fretboard forever.

So, WHY do you need to learn all the notes on the fretboard? Well, in my experience as a teacher, improvisor and instrumentalist focused on guitar, I have seen that finding notes on the fretboard in general, is the thing that slows players down the most.

Whenever you are looking to find the position of a chord or a scale or if you are playing and you want to play a specific note — it seems like the act of locating a note is what holds most players back. And the worst part is, most players don't even notice that this is the thing that's holding them back!

So if you can speed up this entire process, it will change the entire way you play. When you can find your notes faster — the kind of mental process that goes on, the kind of music that you actually play changes for the better. It increases your fluidity. That makes you more musical! And really, isn't that what we all want? To be more musical!

But wait — can't I just learn my fretboard by patterns or intervals instead?
The short answer is "no". Basically — if you are always relying on another note, or location to give you a starting point of reference to find the note you really want- it just slows everything down.
Why would you want to slow yourself down? You don't want to do that!

So, sadly — there are no shortcuts here. You just have to learn all the notes of the fretboard. And really, until you actually learn all the notes on your fretboard — you won't even really "see" what you're missing.

Thankfully the way I'm going to show you how to do this will be fun, easy and you'll memorize your fretboard forever, in just a few minutes a day!
It's really not as hard as you think!

It's actually quite easy!
IF you are willing to practice for 5-15 minutes a day, and you're willing to follow my instructions to the "T"! Even and especially if this is easy for you!

The goal here is not to just learn the notes on the fretboard, but the goal is to make it super fast and seamless so you can get back to making music with your guitar as quickly as possible!
So again — if it's easy — do it anyway!
If it's hard — take it slow!

This system works, you just have to practice these exercises in order, the way I've laid them out.

That's it.

FIRST THINGS FIRST

Here is a diagram of the guitar fretboard this shows you all the natural notes (no sharps or flats) between fret 1 and fret 12. (after that they just repeat) So you just need to learn 12 positions, and they repeat! Kind of like a two for one! Also important to note here is the note names of the open strings.

Now let's get moving on to learning all the notes on the fretboard!

STANDARD TUNED 6 STRING GUITAR

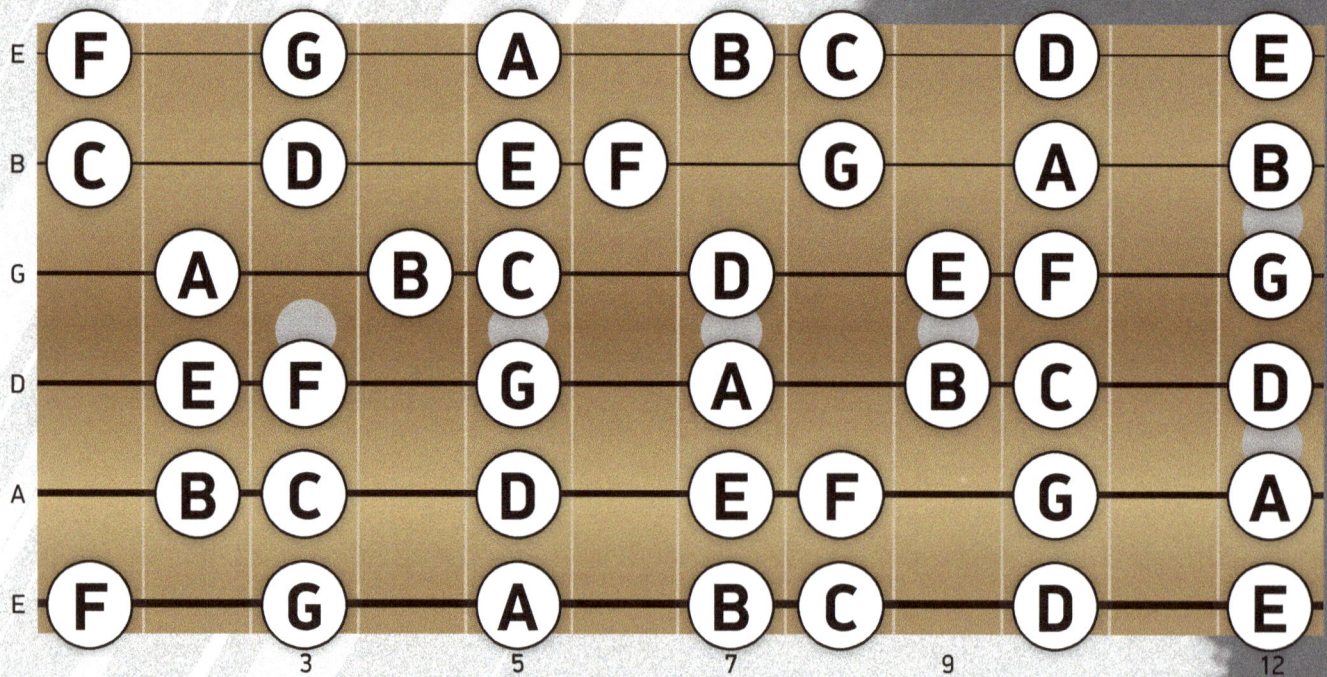

EXERCISE #1

We're going to restrict ourselves to just frets 1 – 12 (since the entire fretboard repeats itself after the 12th fret) We won't use open strings for this. Just fretted notes.

Then decide on a note. It can be any note. But we're only going to choose natural notes, so no sharps, no flats. For demonstration purposes I'll choose A.

STANDARD TUNING

Then we are going to play all of those A notes, in order on every single string. Starting on string 6 and moving up to string 1. Then we'll reverse it.

It's important to remember to do them in order, do not jump strings.

You'll want to be able to achieve this 3 times in a row, with no mistakes.

Once you are able to do this, choose a new note.

! SOME IMPORTANT NOTES TO REMEMBER HERE:
1. Yes — you can keep the diagram(s) in front of you to do this exercise.
2. Don't worry about "memorizing", it's not important for you to memorize the note patterns, it's only important that your hands are playing through the exercise.

! THIS IS VERY IMPORTANT.
3. I suggest setting aside 15 minutes once or twice per day just to do these exercises. This should be separate from your normal practice routine.

That should be enough time to do 3-5 new notes per day. (or eventually all the notes by the time you are done with exercise #1)

The idea is not to simply memorize a pattern — you want to play through the exercise, your muscle memory will do the rest.

Many students become frustrated here, because they can't remember the pattern. That's ok — it's normal. Ignore that feeling and just play the exercise.
Keep playing it.

ABOVE FRET 12 — it's not really necessary to do the exercise above the 12th fret as it literally just repeats what you are doing between frets 1 and 12.
However, if you feel you are less familiar with that section of the fretboard — then you could certainly apply the same exercises to that section of the fret board as well.

DO THIS SAME EXERCISE FOR ALL THE NATURAL NOTES.
(I've included charts in the back of the book for all 12 notes)

Once you can play through all the natural notes twice, flawlessly with no mistakes — you are ready to move onto exercise #2!

EXERCISE #2

We're going to do the same exercise but now we will use a metronome. Set your metronome to **40bpm** and play 1 quarter note per beat.

See the appendix at the end of the book for notation and tablature.

! **IMPORTANT TO NOTE:**
The metronome is **NOT** optional. The metronome is what drives your learning and muscle memory to really internalize these note positions.

40bpm is not very fast, but it's just fast enough to give you something to work at and to give your psyche a little "pressure". It's not enough to make you stress, just to concentrate.

Once you can do exercise #2 for all the natural notes cleanly at 40bpm, you are ready for exercise #3!

STANDARD TUNING

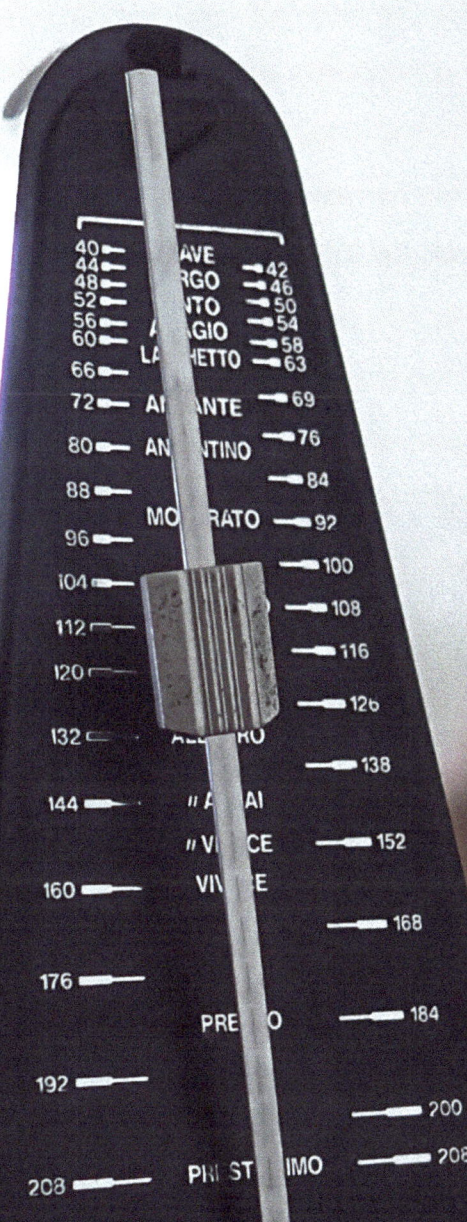

EXERCISE #3

We're going to add all the accidentals
(all the sharps and flats).
(There is an appendix at the back of the book for all the notation/tablature/charts)

Here's a diagram of all the sharps.

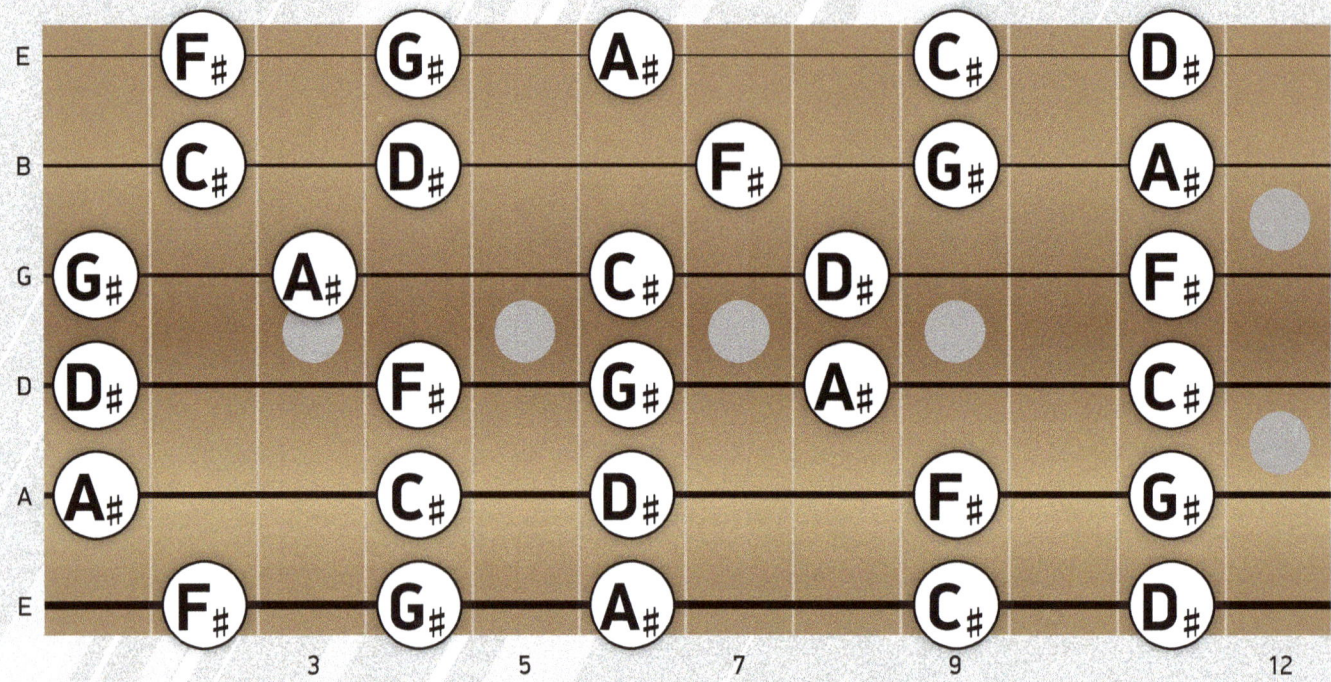

> **! SOMETHING IMPORTANT TO NOTE:**
> I've only shown the sharps on the above diagram but those same locations are also flats!

Because of Enharmonic equivalence you can call the note one or the other. It doesn't really matter except for harmonic analyzation purposes, which is a super specific academic pursuit and that we don't have time for in this book!

Typically, when I think of ascending the neck, I tend to think in sharps. When I'm descending I tend to think in flats. You can choose whichever you like. Just know that they are the same note locations.

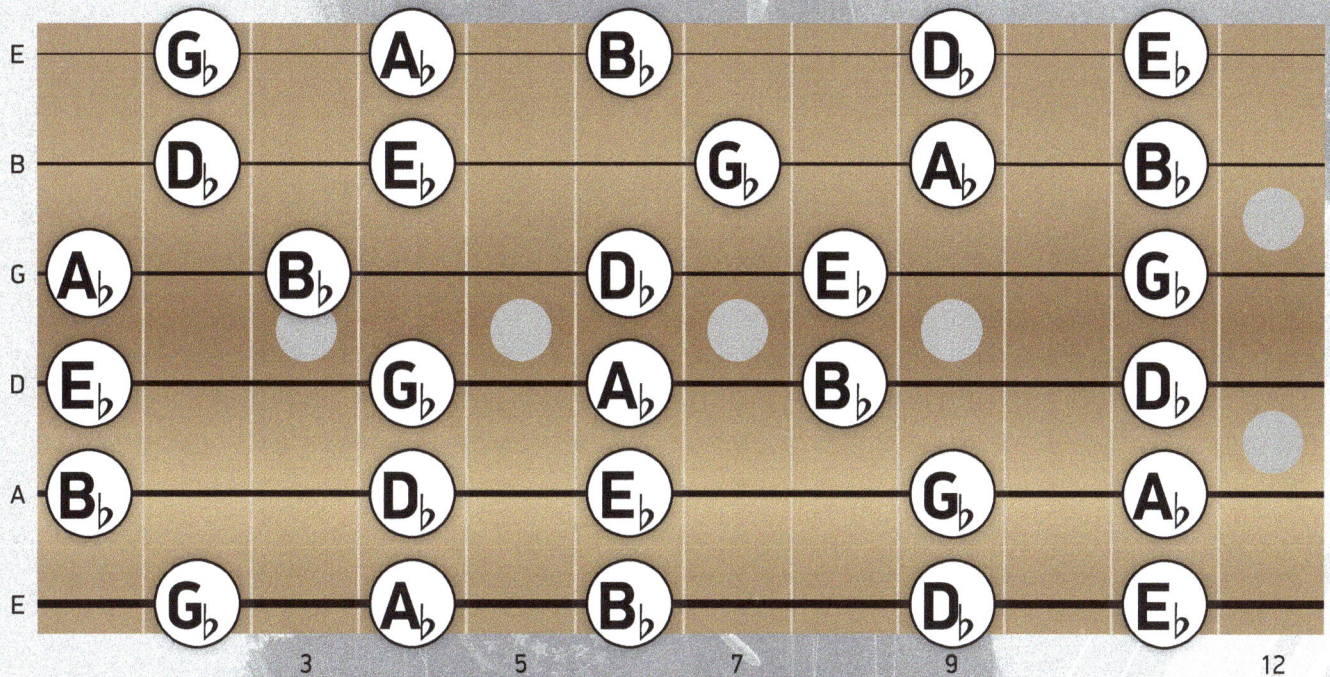

Here's that same diagram but this time showing flats.

Once you can do all the sharps/flats, cleanly, with no mistakes at least twice through with a metronome at 40bpm you'll be ready to move on to exercise #4.

EXERCISE #4

For this exercise we choose 2 notes to practice at a time. It doesn't matter which you choose, and you can mix natural notes and accidentals.
It doesn't really matter.

Once you've chosen your notes — you play 1 note up and the other note going down.

No stopping when you get to the top. Just immediately play the next note and descend, no stopping.

You should be doing this with a metronome still set to 40bpm. I know it's slow — but trust me, you want to keep it slow for now!

Here is an example for you using G# and C.

STANDARD TUNING

After you've practiced all 12 notes in pairs and when this gets easy for you — you are now ready to move on to exercise #5

EXERCISE #5

7 notes in random order!

It doesn't matter which notes you choose, you can use naturals and accidentals.
We're expanding on exercise 4.

So let's choose: D, F#,C, E, A#,G, B

You'll ascend on D, descend on F#, ascend on C, descend on E, ascend on A# descend on G and ascend on B.
No stopping, clean and fluid throughout at 40 bpm.
Until all the notes of the fretboard have been played through in this manner.

Example:

STANDARD TUNING

Once you have played through all the notes in this way, cleanly and without stopping at 40bpm and it feels EASY — then it's finally time to move on to Exercise #6

EXERCISE #6

You will repeat all the exercises from #2 – 5 with the metronome increasing the speed.
Your goal speed will be **80bpm.**

Once you can do all the exercises cleanly, without stopping at 80bpm — you're done!

That's it — it's magic!

THAT'S A WRAP!

That's it. We're done!
There's really not much more to say. This book is a very purpose written, singular-goal oriented, system for you to learn the fretboard— painlessly and forever!

If you follow this simple 6 step exercise series: you'll have the fretboard memorized in no time at all! I'm not going to make any outlandish claims like "you'll be able to memorize the fretboard in 24 hours", although I think that's a reasonable goal. (To be honest, I feel that 24 hours in total spread out over about a 1 – 2 week period is more than sufficient for this goal.)

The truth is — most, if not all, the books already on the market teach you the "L Shape Rule"; "The Octave Trick"; "Chromatic Counting" and "Mnemonic Devices" to memorize the note locations and how the fretboard fits together, but none of these methods truly help you or force you to actually memorize note locations. They are simply tricks and "memory hacks" to help you locate notes. But as I mentioned in the introduction — there are no shortcuts here. You just have to learn all the notes of the fretboard. And really, until you actually learn all the notes on your fretboard — you won't even really "see" what you're missing.

The reality is that you can have a perfectly fine time of learning the guitar and all of your scales, modes, chords and shapes by simply memorizing the note locations on the lowest couple of strings, and all of the associated patterns that go with them. However, to truly learn and master the instrument— you need to dig just a little deeper and truly commit to learning the fundamentals. I'll even go so far as to utilize the old architecture metaphor: If you don't have a solid foundation for your house, it will never be truly strong.

Learning the notes on the fretboard is that foundation to your guitar "house"!
If you never do it— you'll never know the benefit. But if you put in your time— I promise that you will start to understand not only the guitar better, but music, theory and life itself! (ok, maybe not that last one...but a guy can dream right?)

I can only write a book, and make videos, and put out social media posts, I can't physically make you do these exercises or in fact spend any time at all learning your instrument. Only you can do that. If you don't want to do it, you won't. If you DO want to do it, you will. It's that simple.

APPENDIX

NATURAL NOTES ON THE FRETBOARD

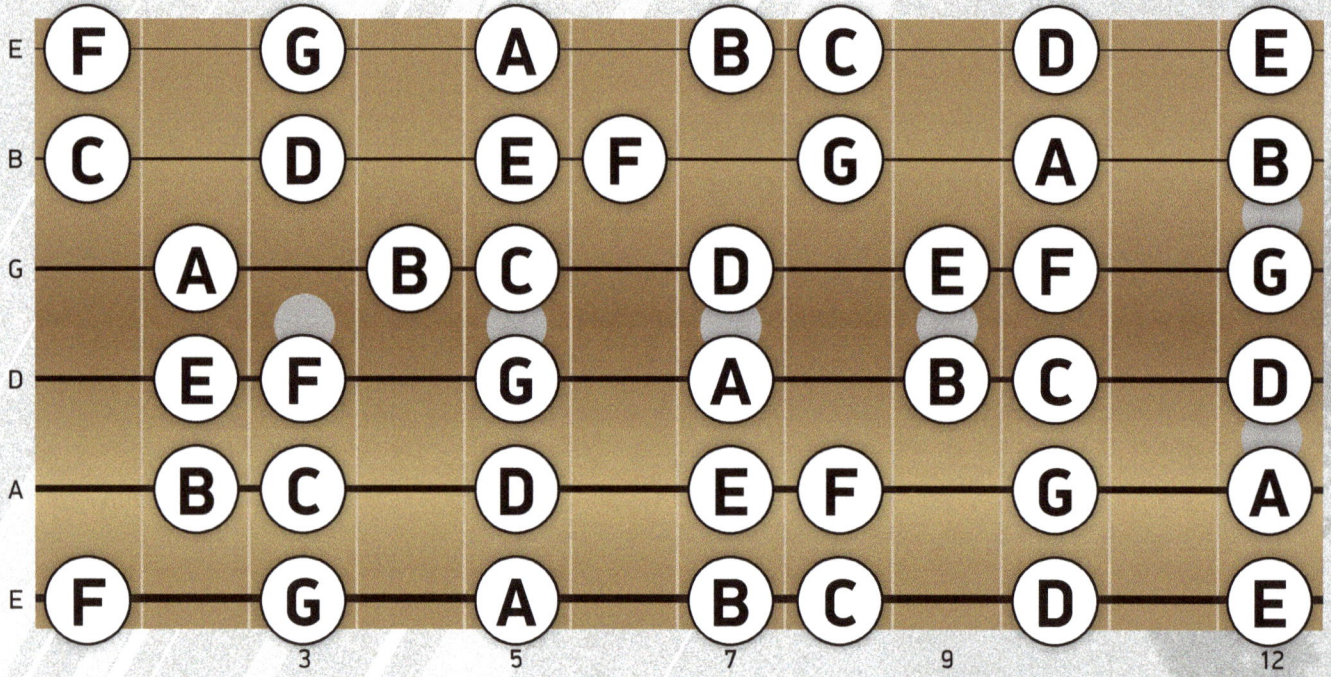

SHARPS/FLATS ON THE FRETBOARD

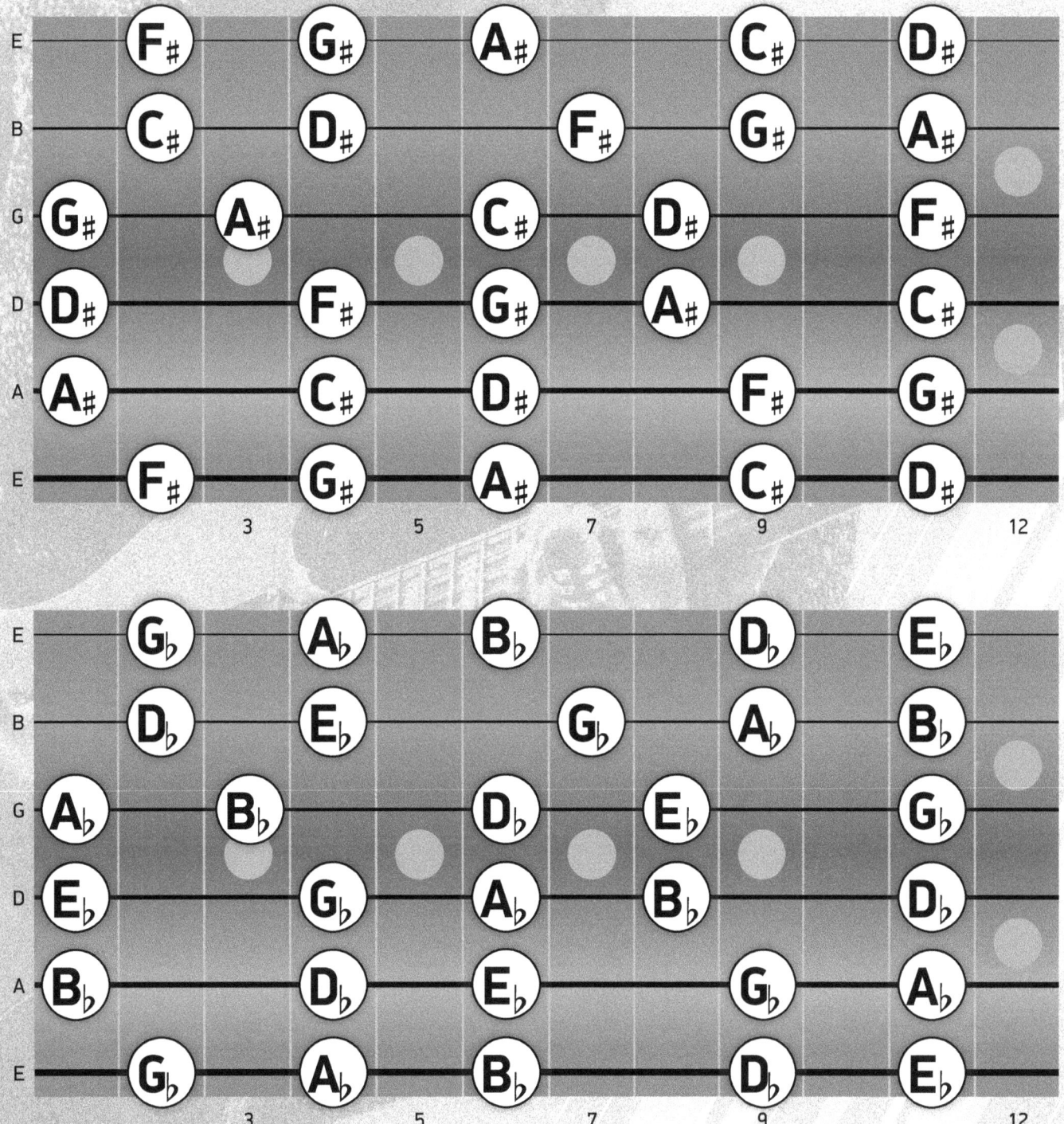

APPENDIX

NOTE LOCATIONS

A

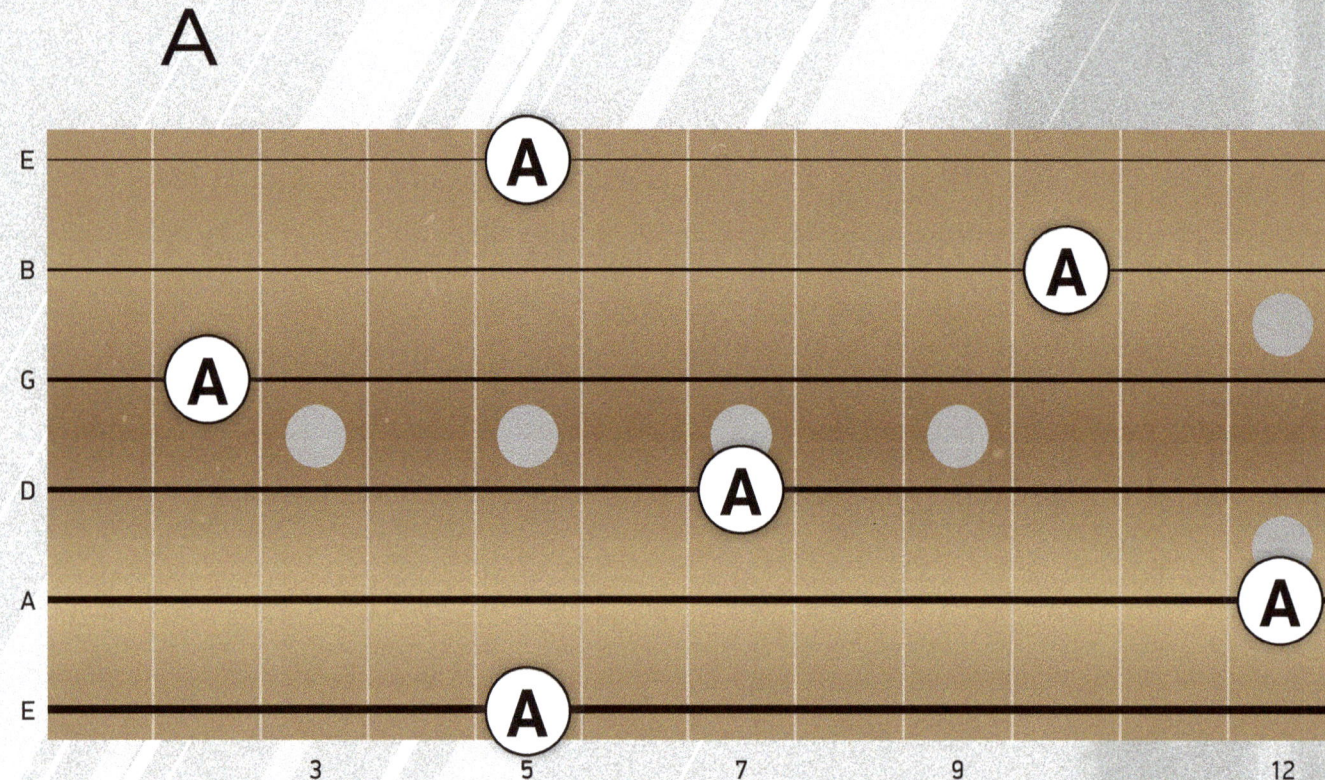

A#

String	3	5	7	9	12
E			A#		
B					A#
G	A#				
D				A#	
A	A#				
E			A#		

APPENDIX

NOTE LOCATIONS:

B

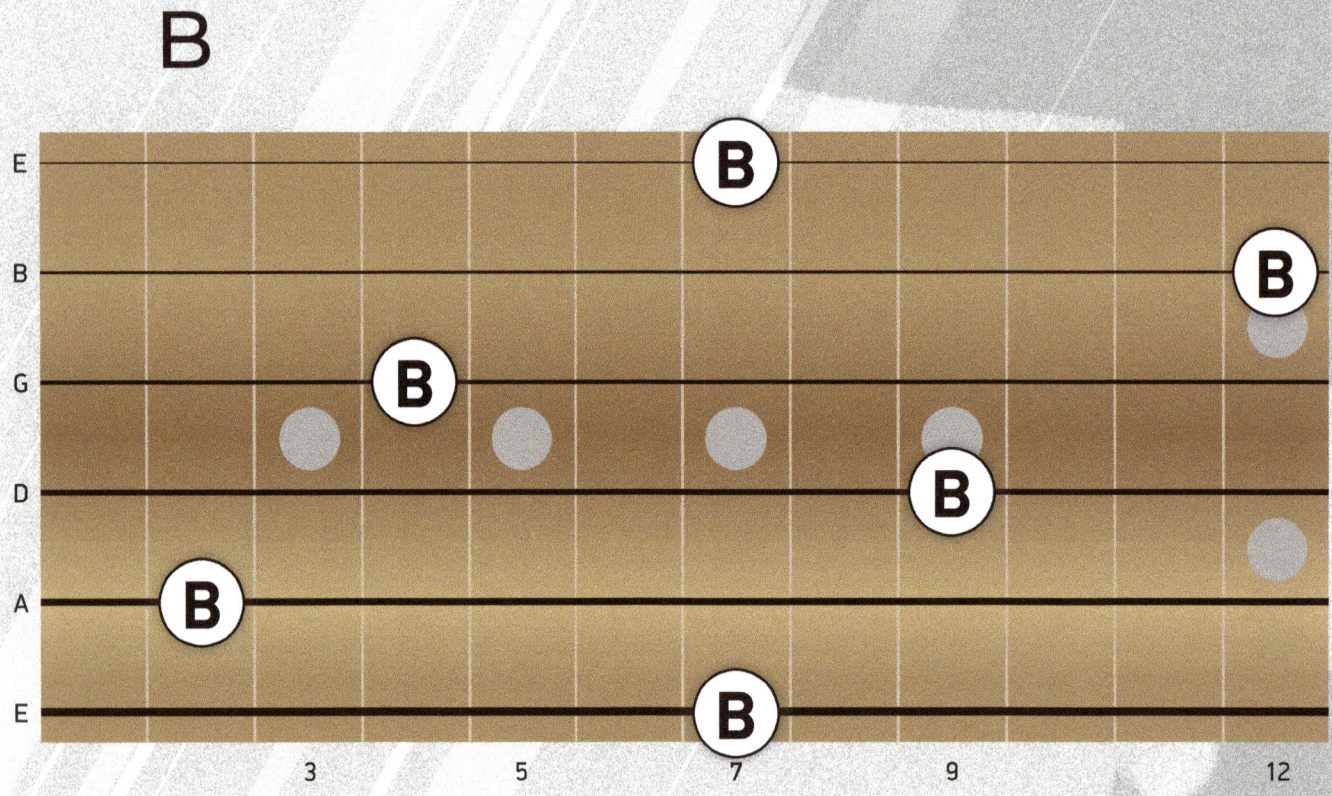

APPENDIX

NOTE LOCATIONS:

C

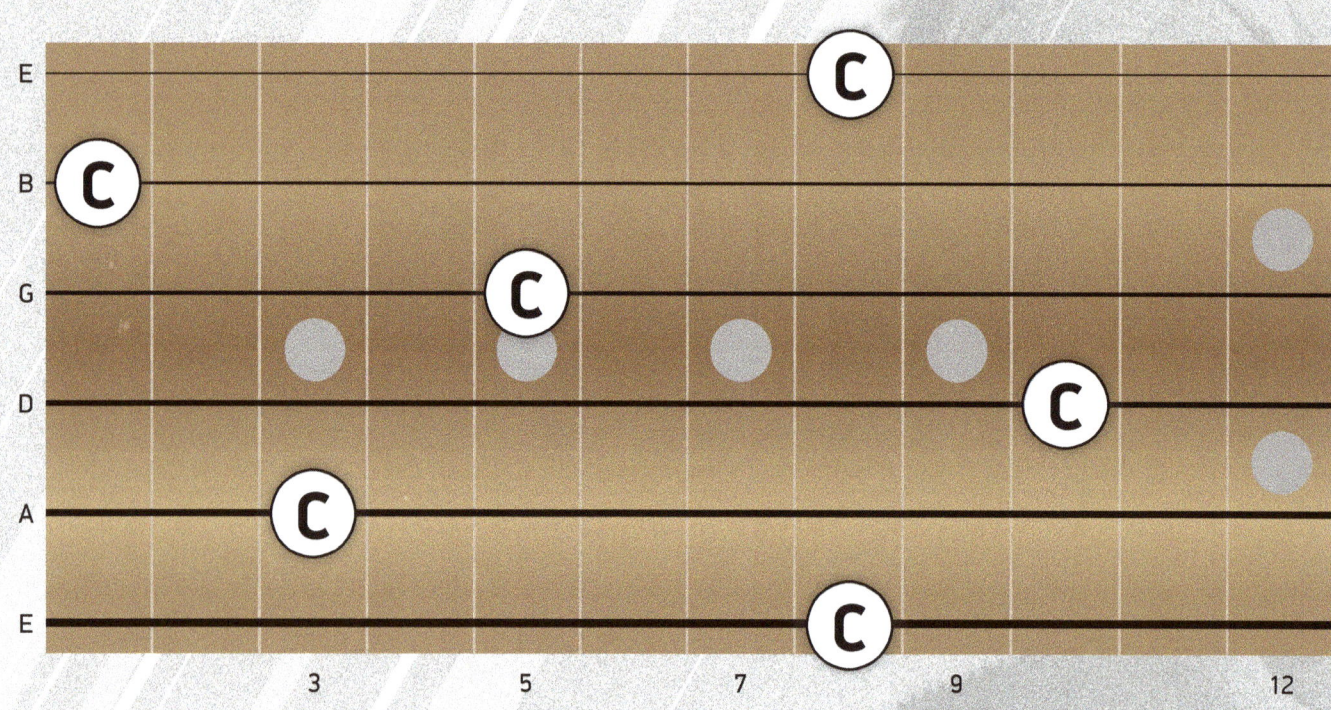

C#

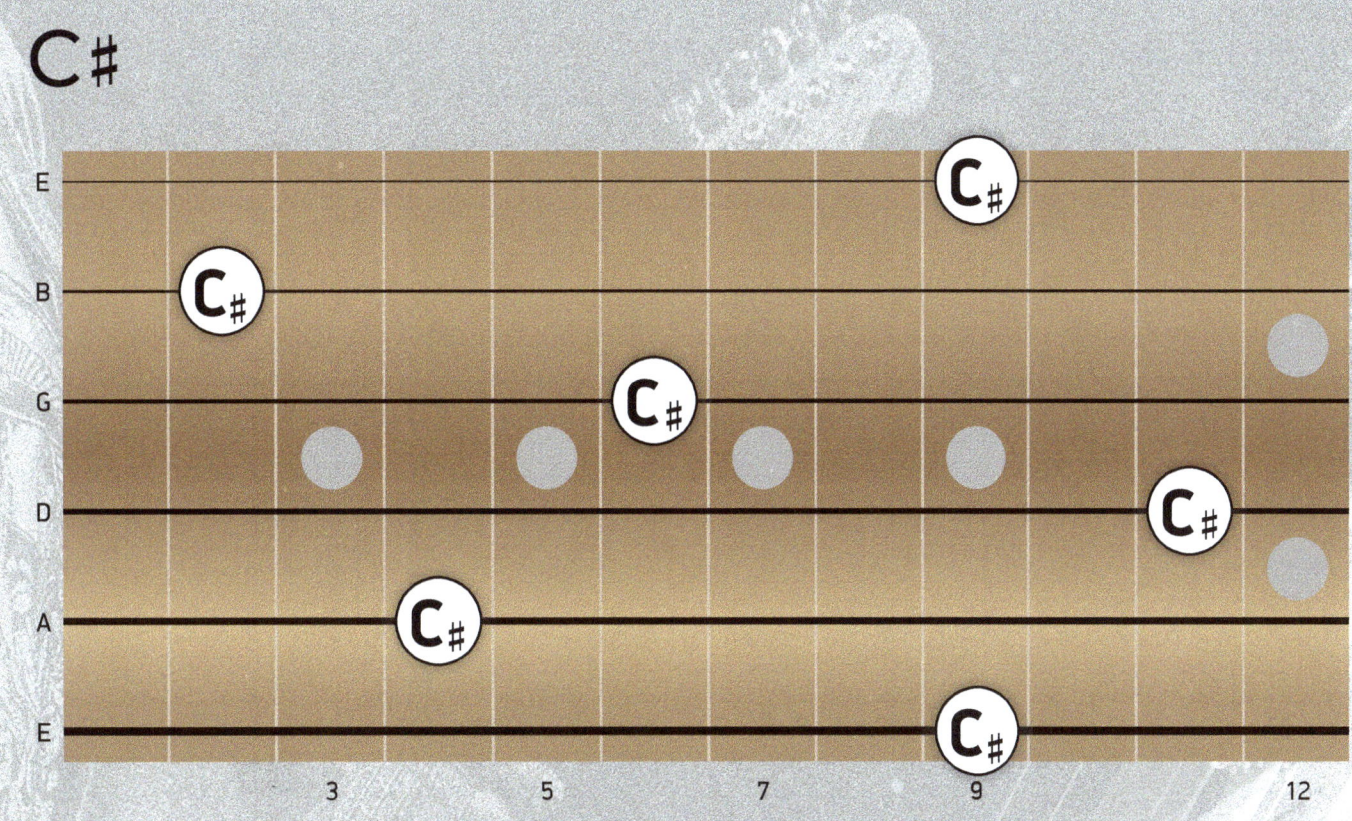

APPENDIX

NOTE LOCATIONS:

D

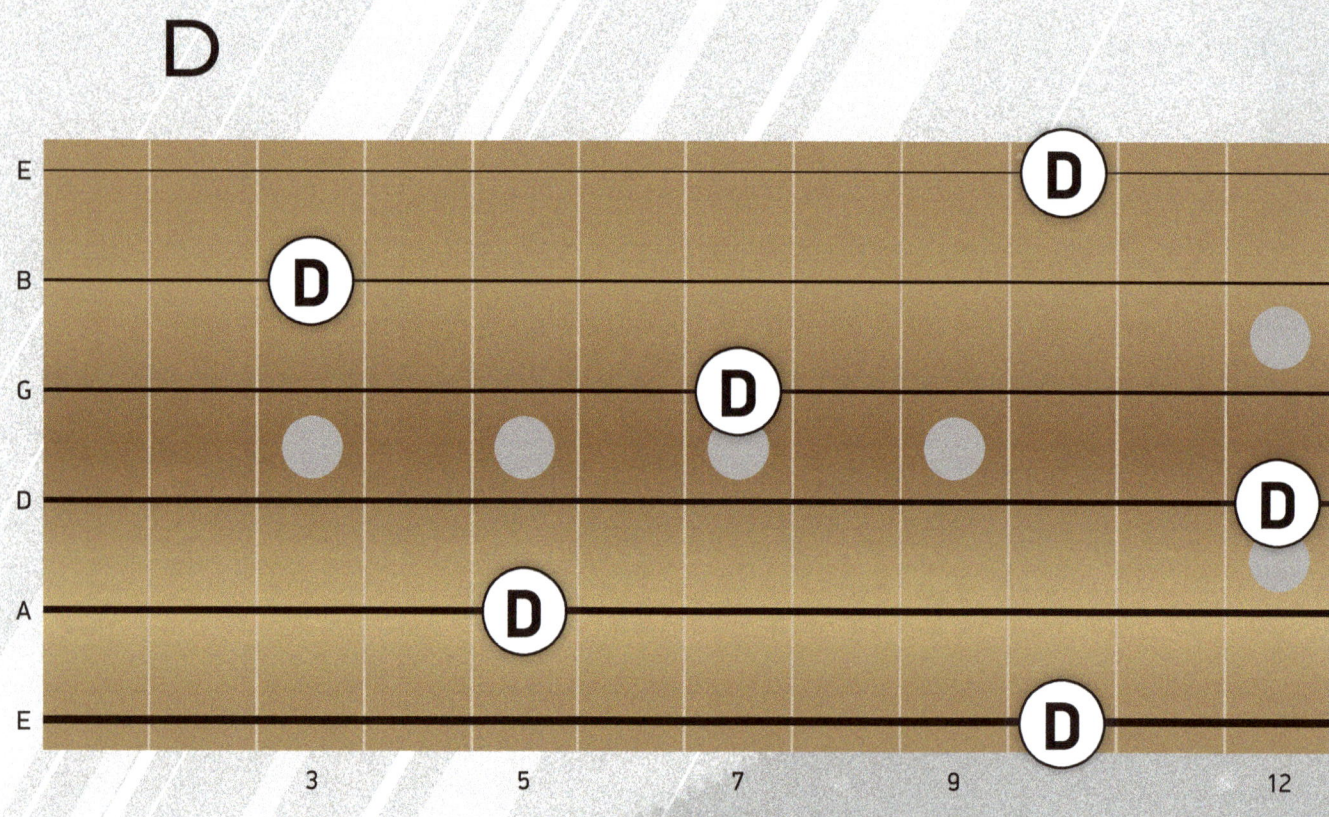

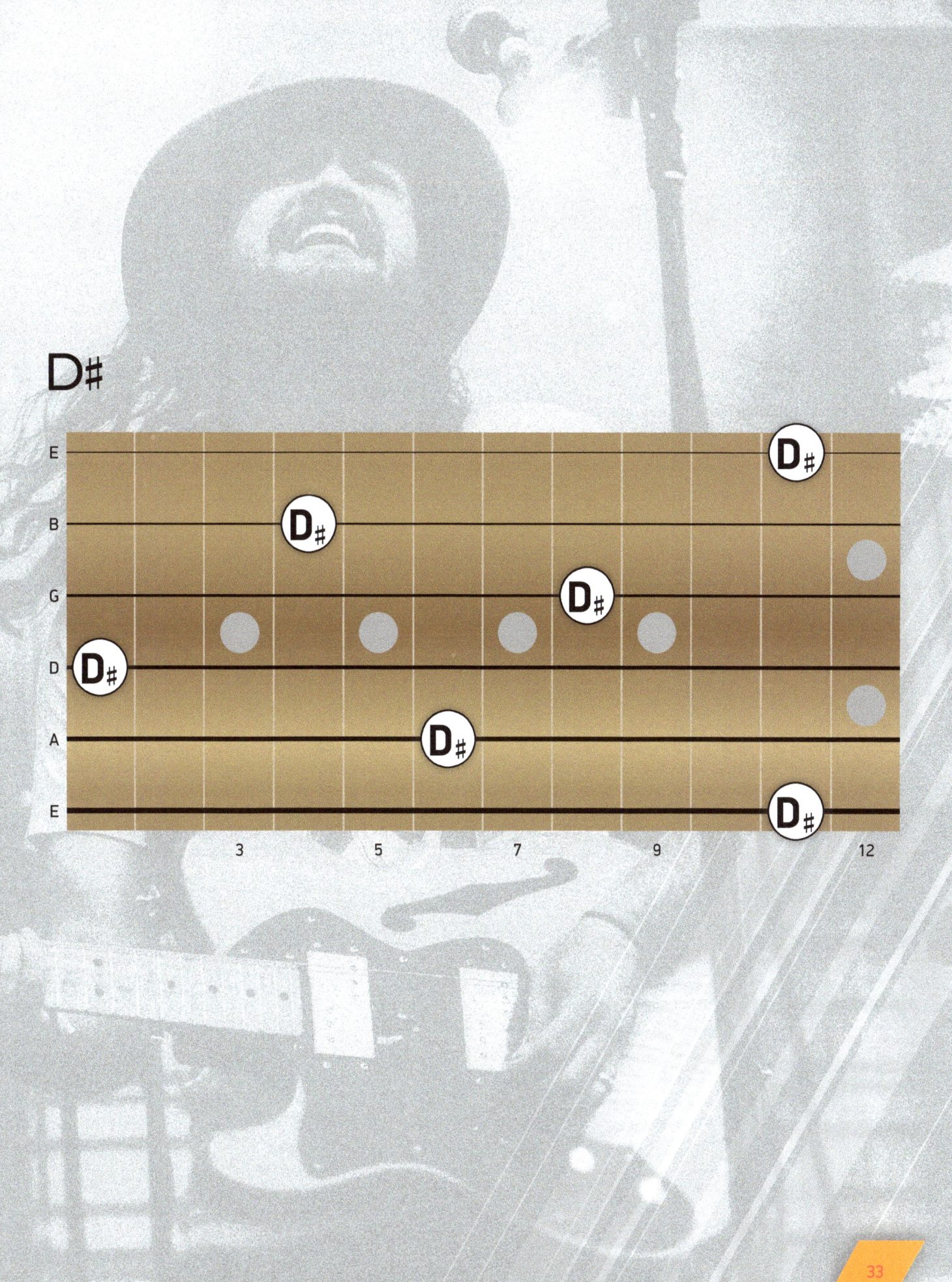

APPENDIX

NOTE LOCATIONS:

E

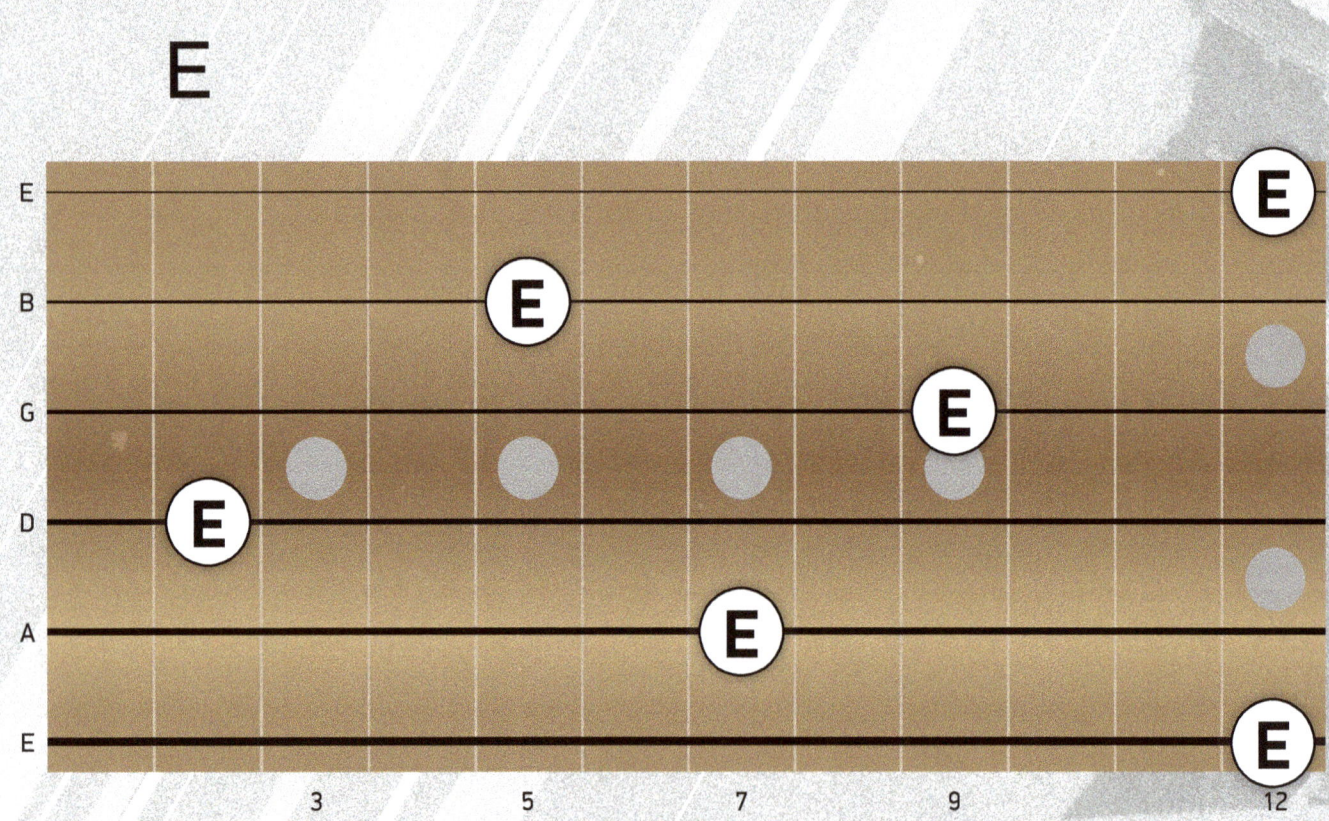

APPENDIX

NOTE LOCATIONS:

F

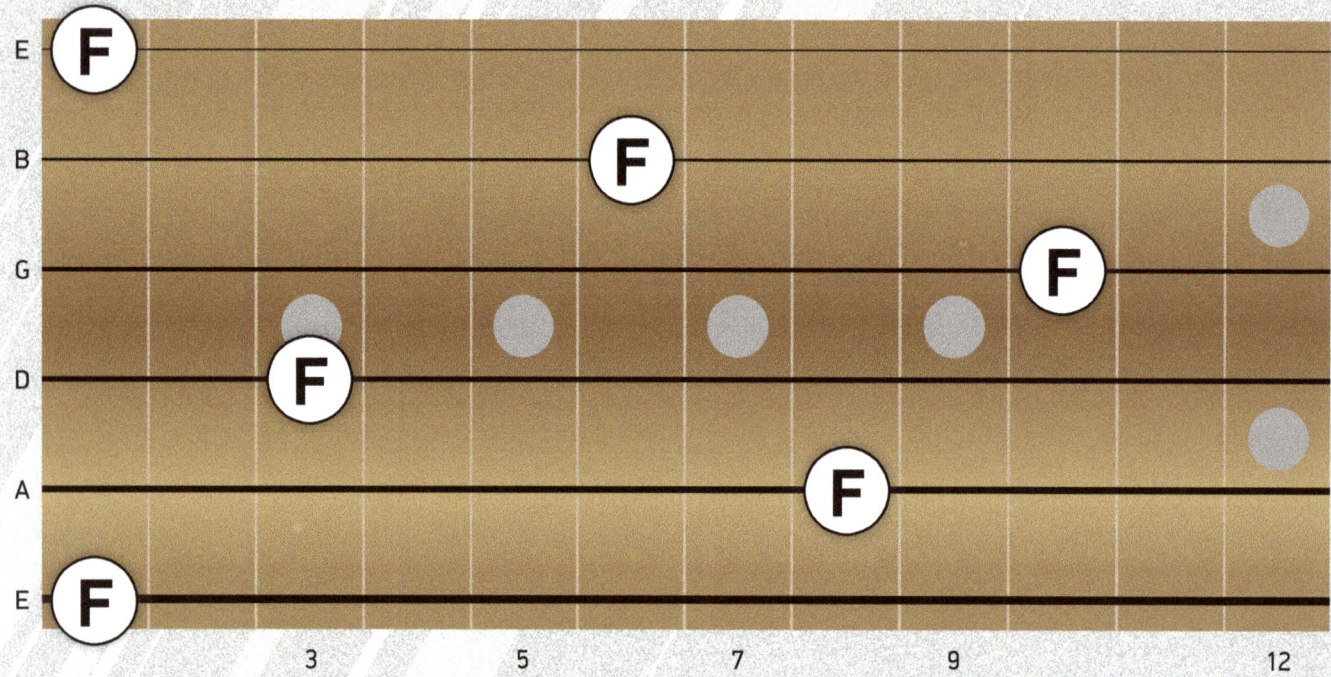

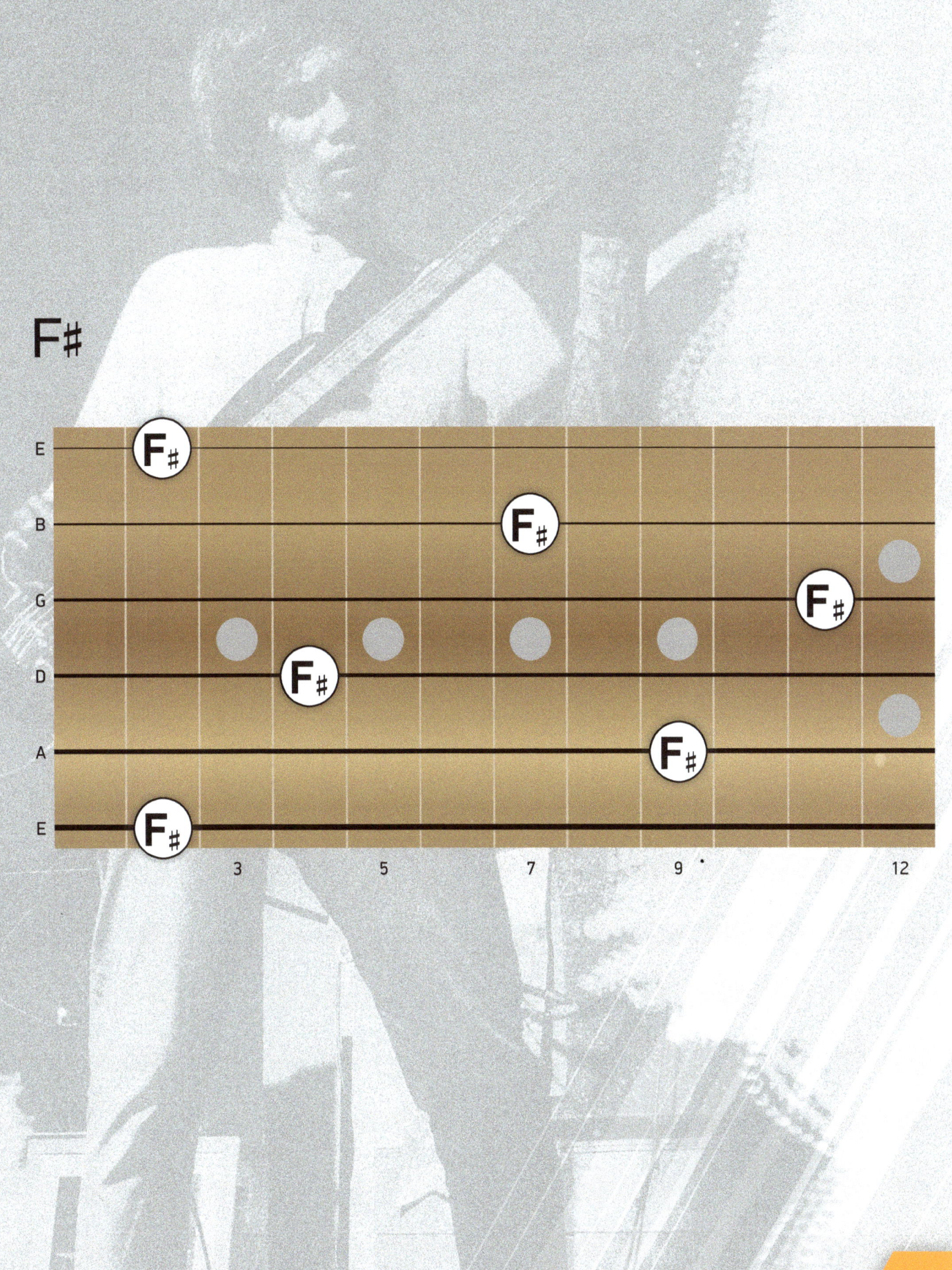

APPENDIX

NOTE LOCATIONS:

G

G#

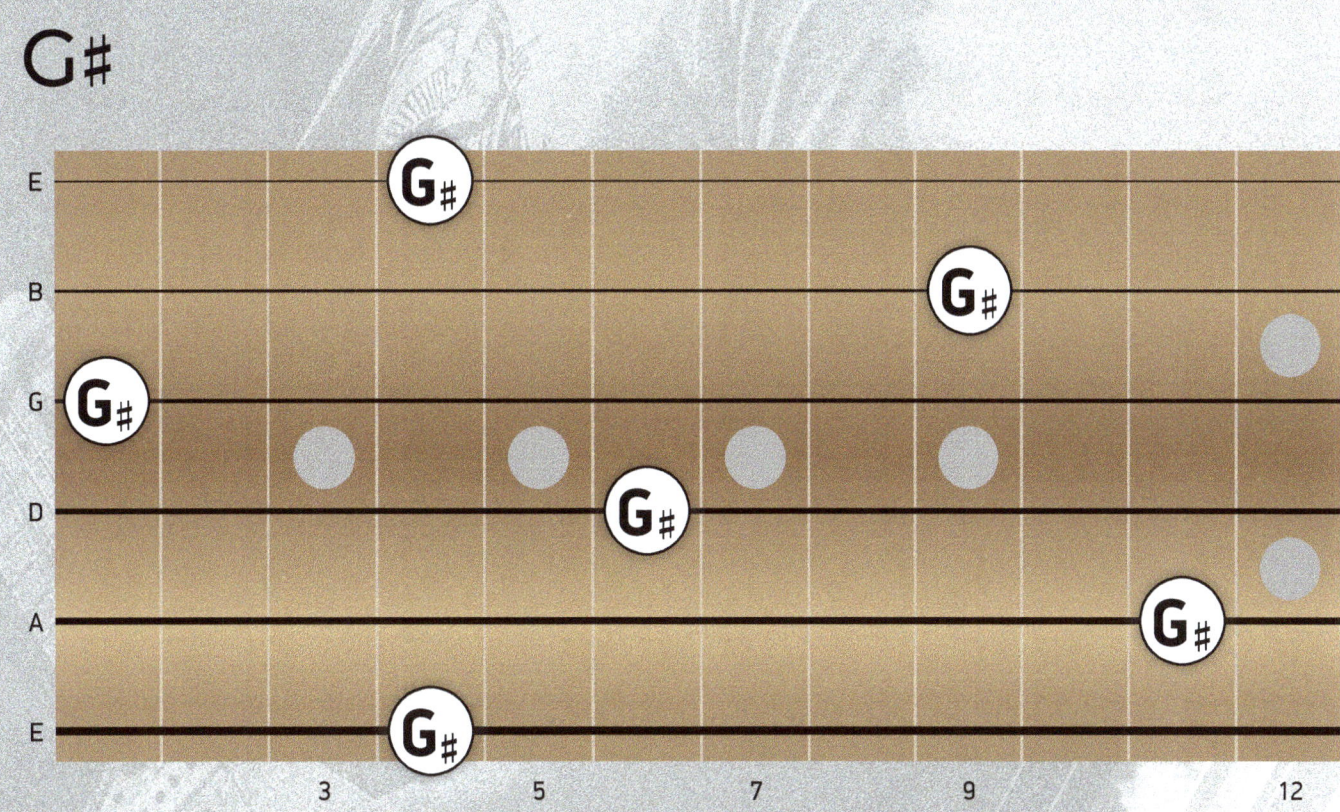

APPENDIX

BLANK CHORD DIAGRAMS FOR YOUR USE

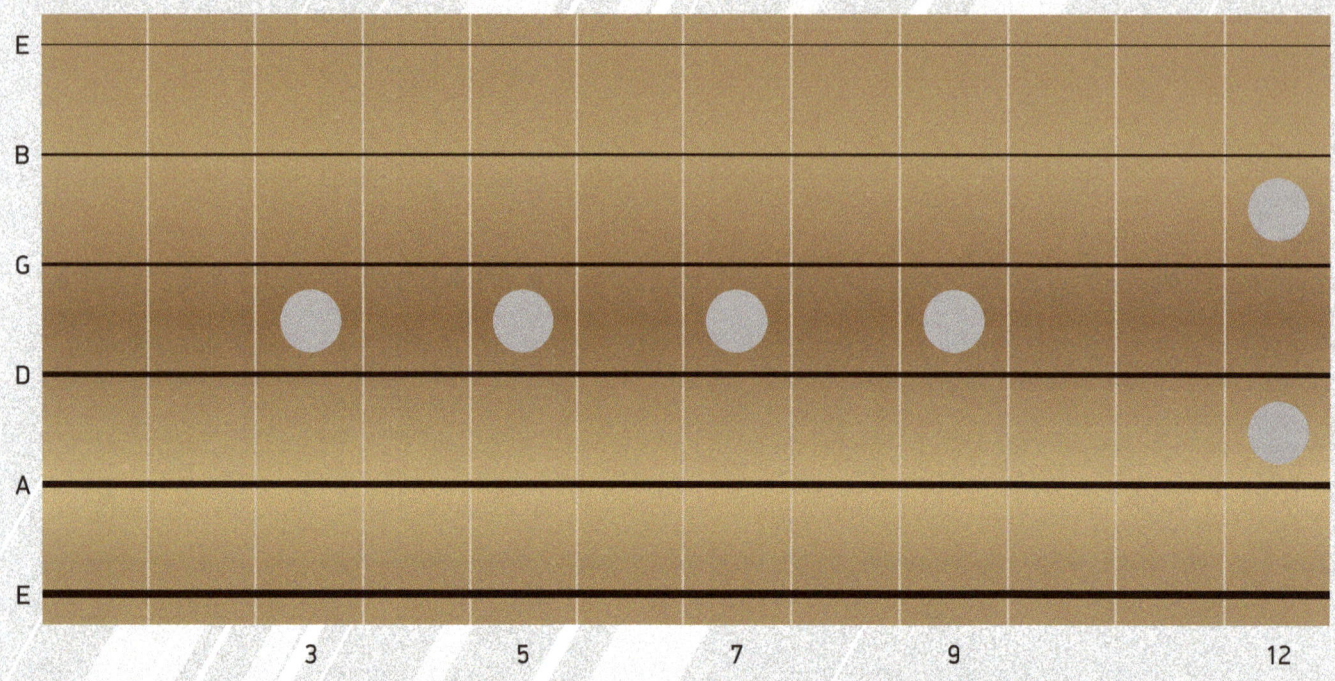

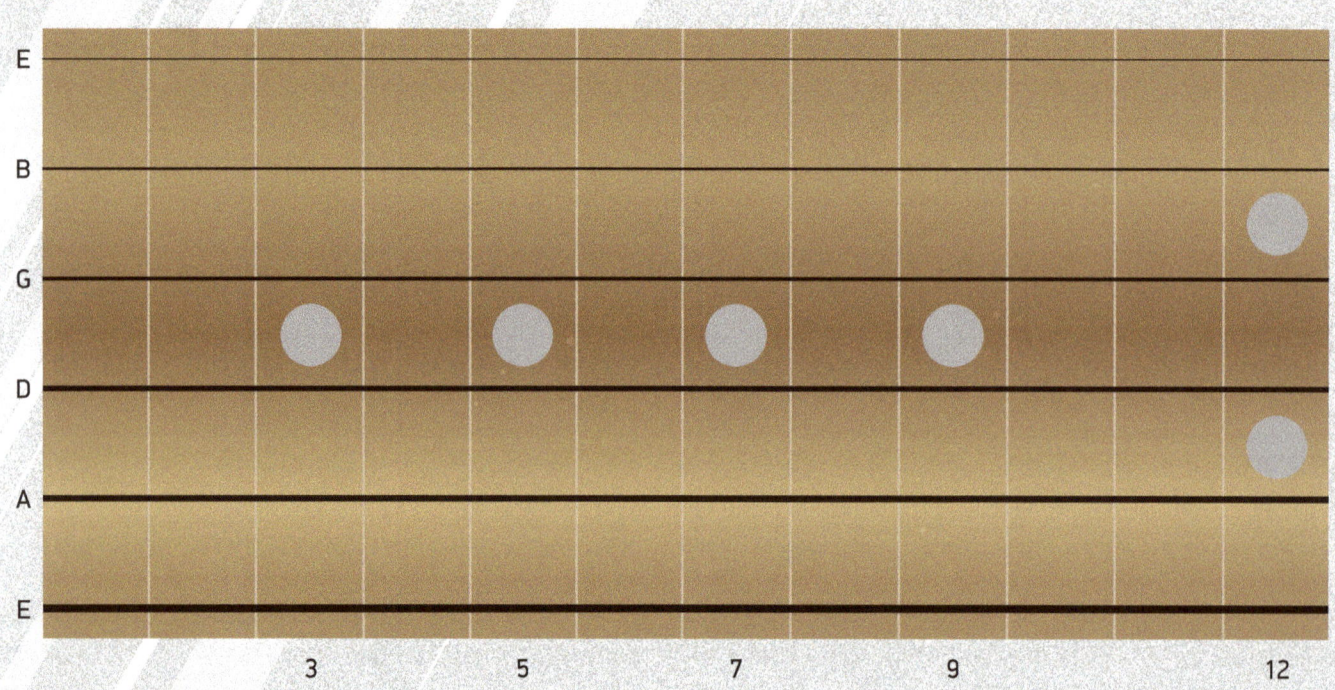

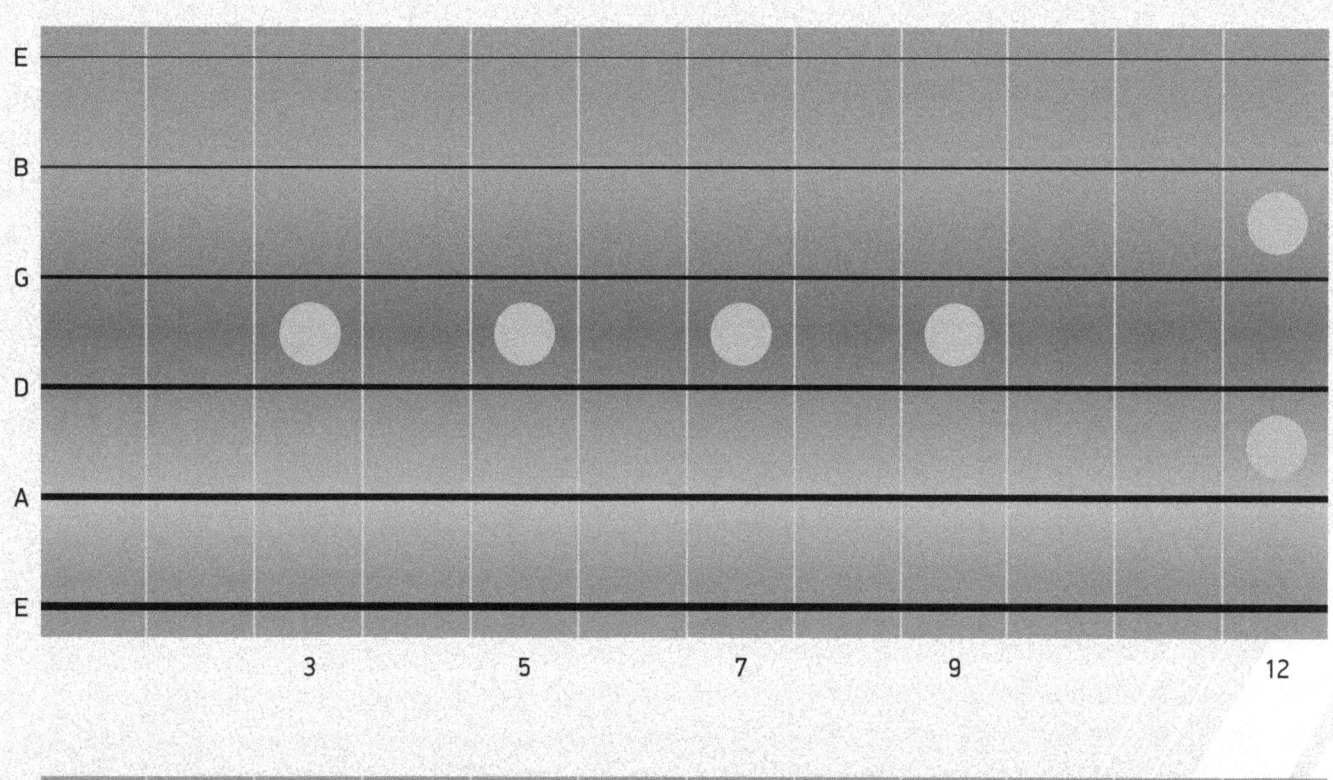
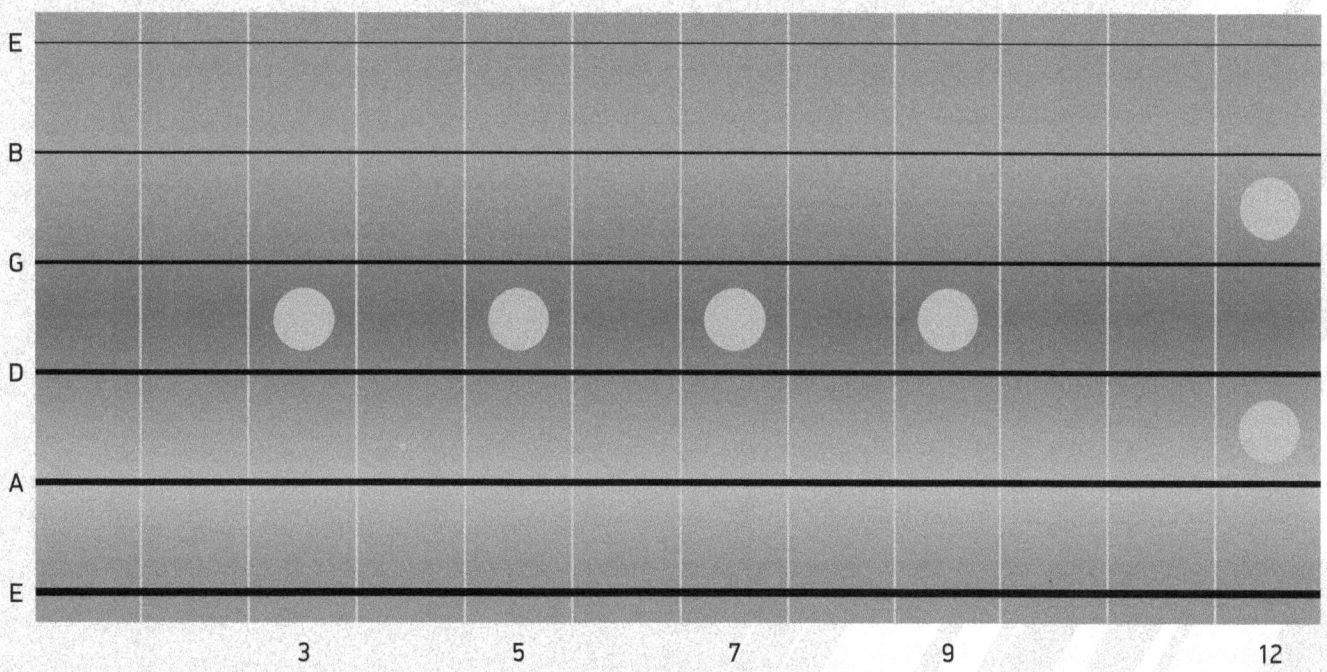

APPENDIX

BLANK CHORD DIAGRAMS FOR YOUR USE

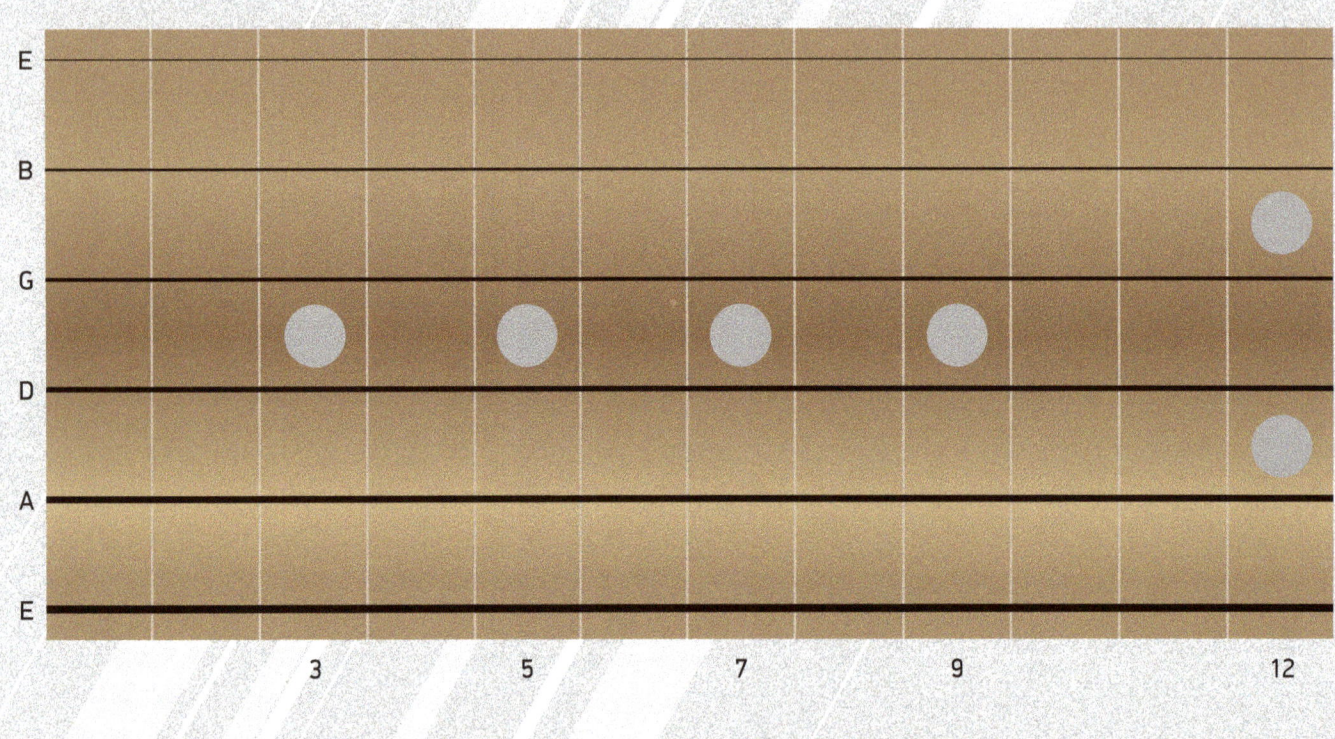

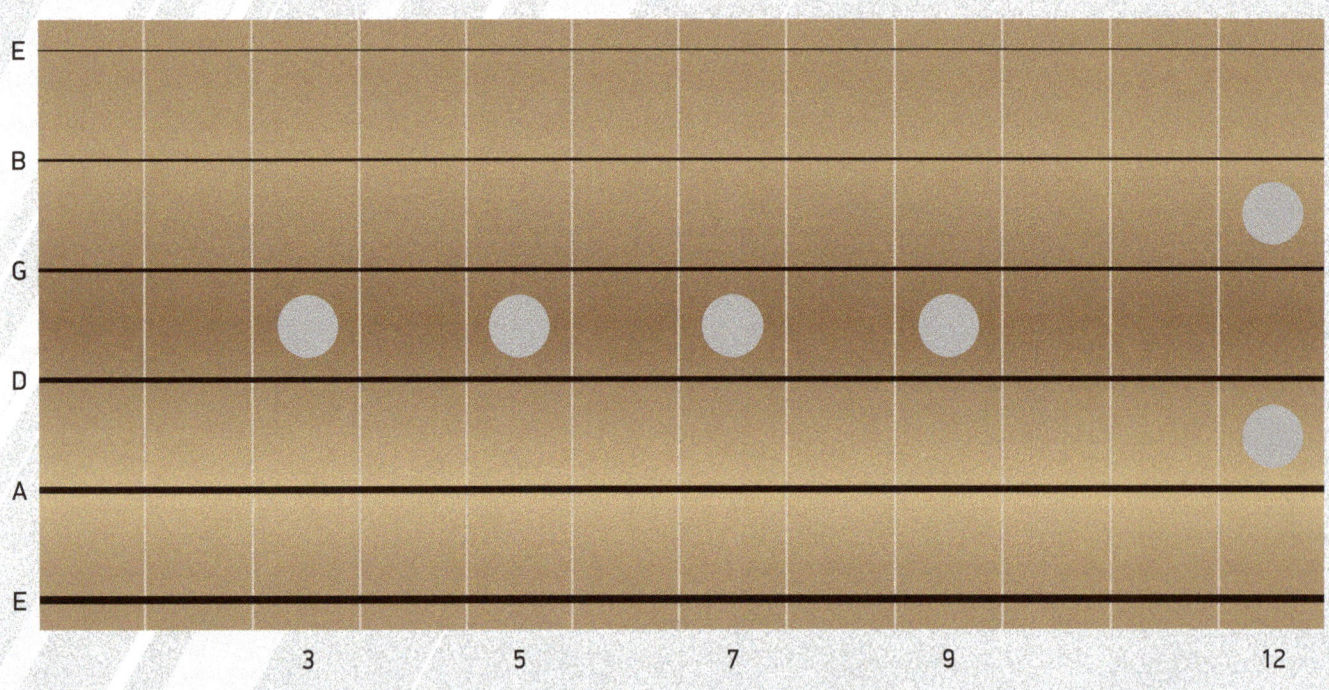

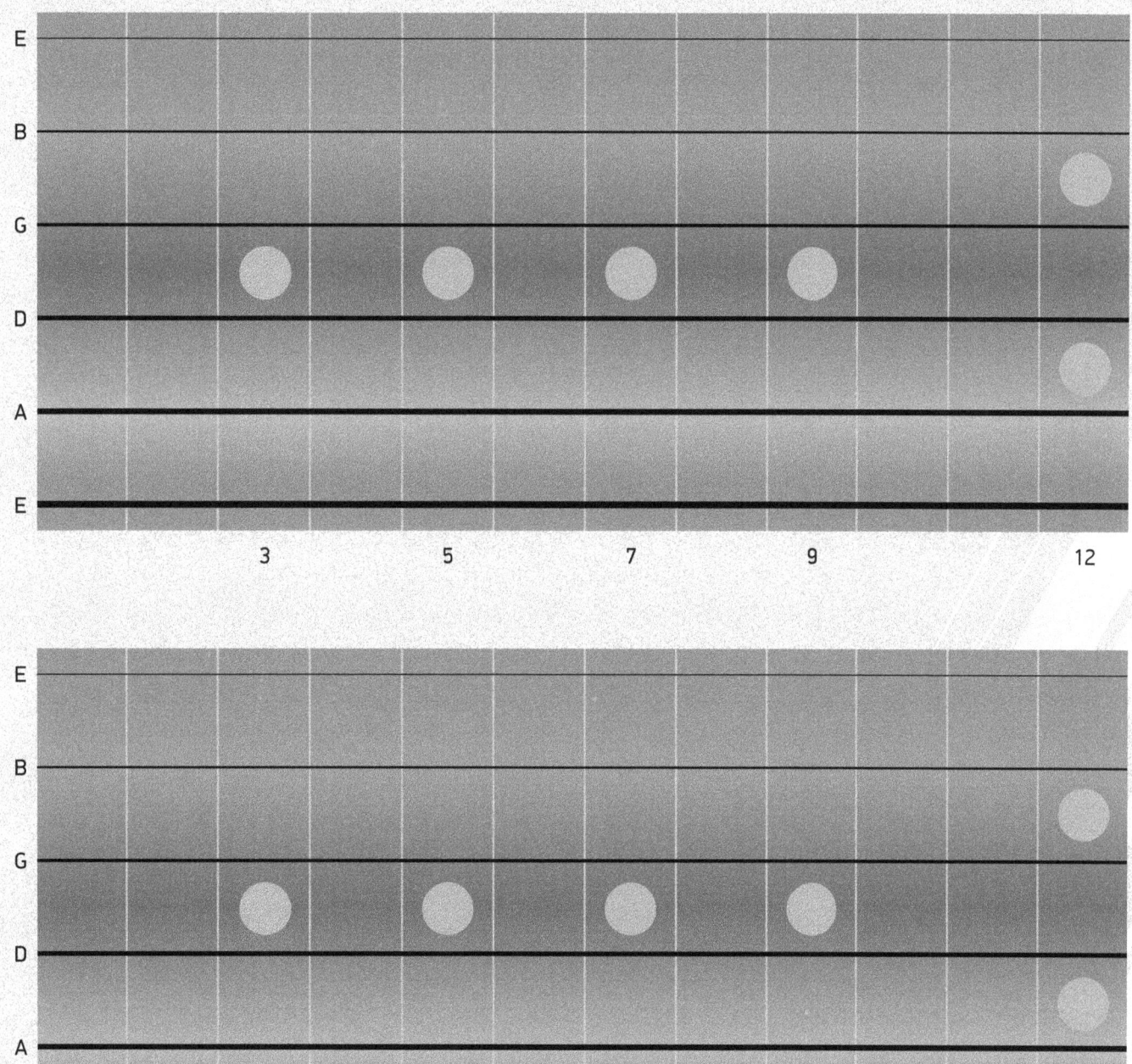

APPENDIX

BLANK CHORD DIAGRAMS FOR YOUR USE

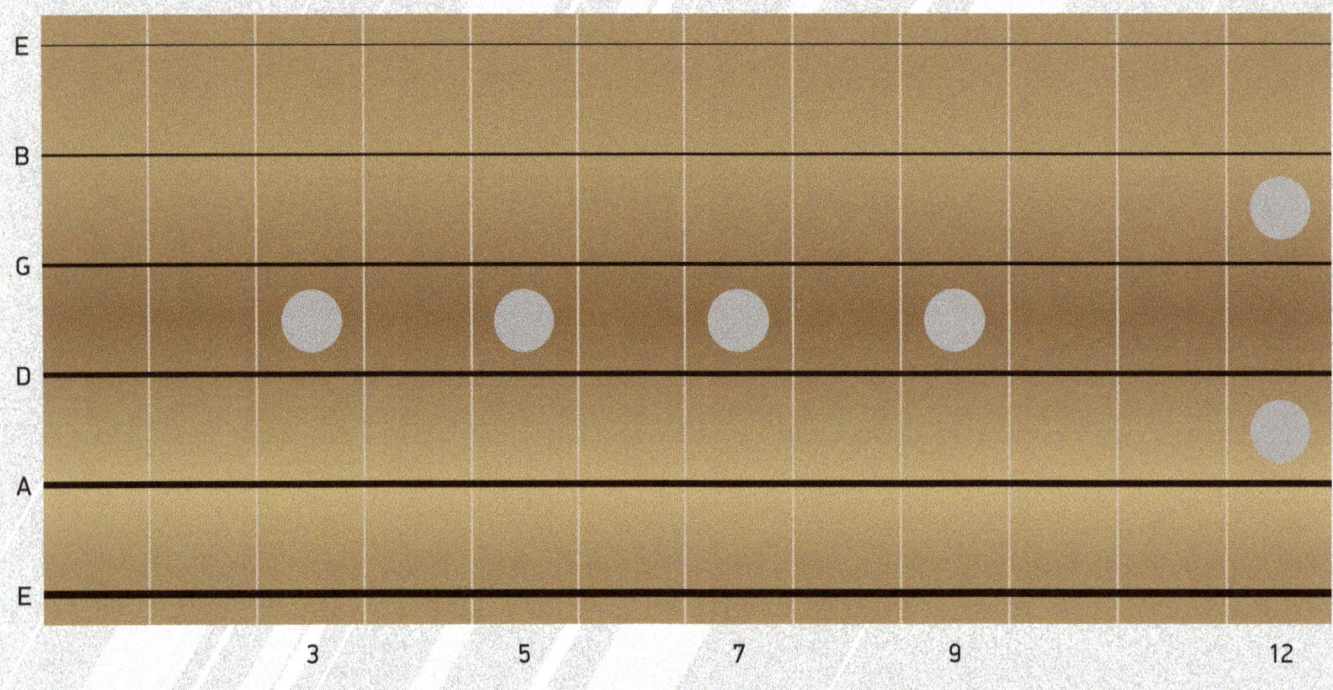

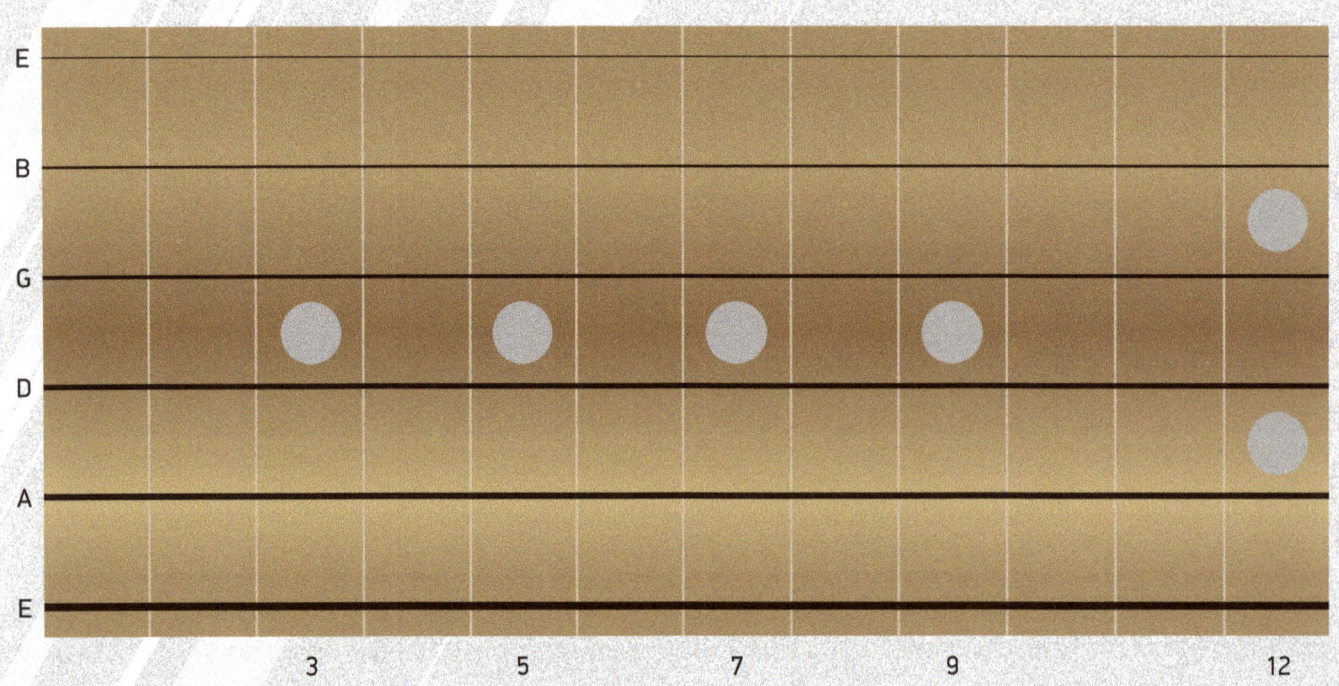

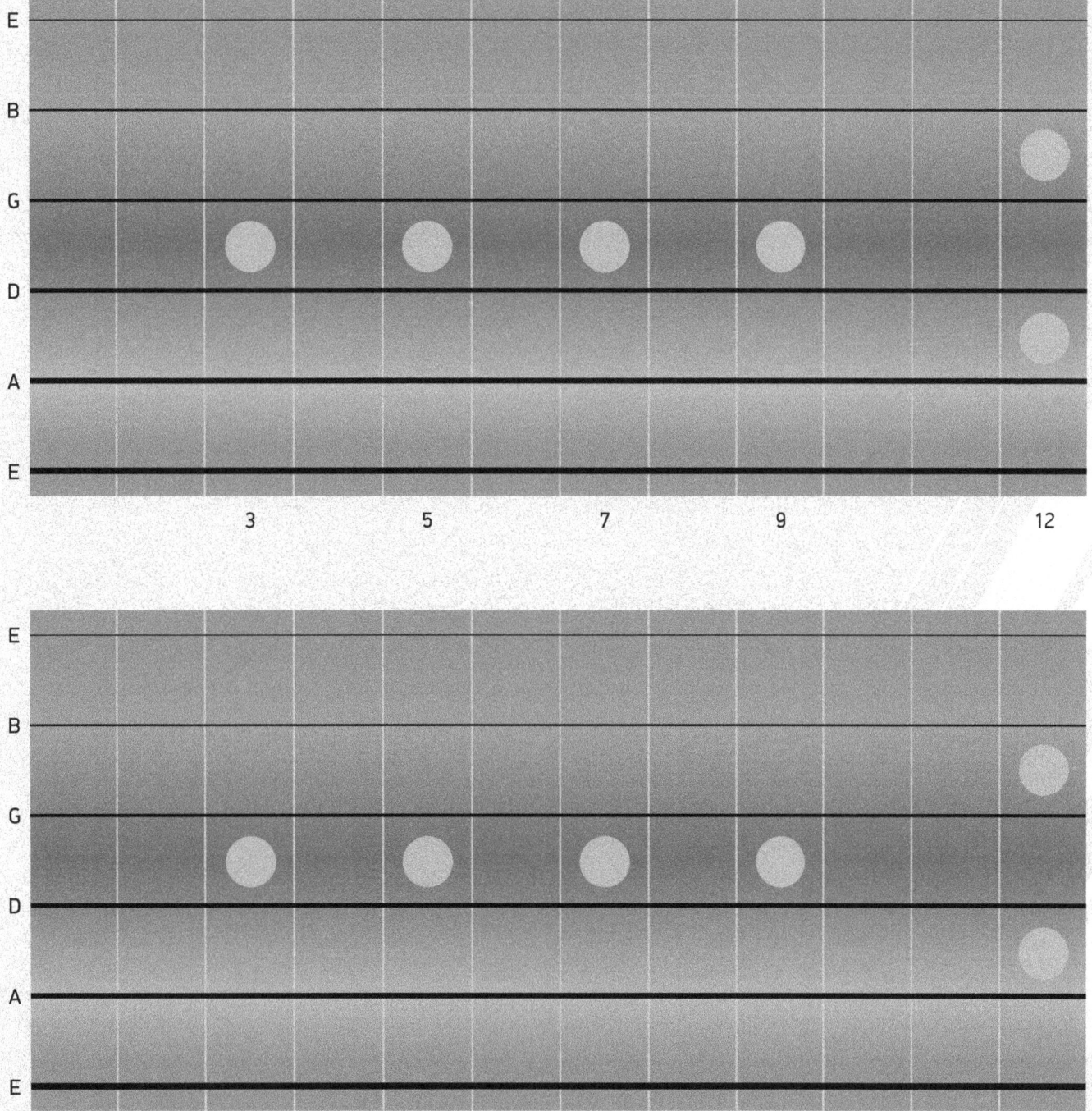

APPENDIX

BLANK STAFF/TAB PAPER FOR YOUR USE

APPENDIX

BLANK STAFF/TAB PAPER FOR YOUR USE

APPENDIX

BLANK STAFF/TAB PAPER FOR YOUR USE

APPENDIX

BLANK STAFF/TAB PAPER FOR YOUR USE

FINAL NOTE

That is where I'll leave you now.
It's up to you!
You have the power in your hands —
what will you do with it?

If I can ever be of any help, feel free to reach out to me in the Facebook Group, or via email at: nick@guitardojo.ca

Here's to your success!

Yours,
Nick Morrison

P.S. If you found this book helpful, if it really did help you, if you were really able to memorize the fretboard quickly and painlessly — I would truly, genuinely, and humbly ask that you leave me a review on Amazon.

As an independent publisher the only way I can compete with Hal Leonard or Mel Bay is with reviews. If passionate fans like you take just a few minutes and leave an open and honest review on Amazon — it shows their algorithm that real people are buying and liking my books, which in turn allows them to promote my book to other potential readers and help to grow the guitar playing community.

GD2021-WCE15P

GUITAR FRETBOARD
MEMORY MAGIC

PAINLESSLY MEMORIZE ALL THE NOTES ON YOUR NECK FOREVER FOR INSTANT RECALL

Why Would I Want to Learn All the Notes of My Fretboard?

Over my 25+ year career as a musician and guitar teacher, I have come across many guitarists who cannot name all the frets on the fretboard. Learning the guitar or music theory for that matter, with no knowledge of the basic fundamental organization of the fretboard is a bit like trying to learn to swim without getting into the water. While not impossible, it just doesn't make a much sense! This book will make sure you don't wind up like countless other guitar players who can't name the most basic building blocks on their instruments — the notes!

Here's why you should learn the fretboard:
- Understand how the instrument is arranged for melodic and harmonic application
- Create a mind map that lets you navigate the fretboard seamlessly and quickly
- Helps to communicate musical ideas to the written form much faster
- Creates a deeper bond with your instrument

Here's What You'll Find Inside:
- The easiest system of learning the fretboard, organized into 6 easy exercises
- A step by step approach that will give you results, fast and painlessly
- All the charts and notation/tabs to show you exactly what to do
- Beginner friendly — no prior music theory experience necessary!
- Blank tab charts and chord diagrams to design your own versions of the exercises!

So what are you waiting for? Start your guitar learning journey now!
Or simply continue your journey and make your guitar practice even more satisfying!

NICK MORRISON
WWW.GUITARDOJO.CA

www.ingramcontent.com/pod-product-compliance
Lightning Source LLC
Chambersburg PA
CBHW051258110526

44589CB00025B/2875